# The Outhouse Book

## by Wayne Allred

### Illustrated by David Mecham

• A WILLOW TREE BOOK •

Published by:
Willow Tree Books
Box 640
Roy, Utah
84067-0640

ISBN 1-885027-07-9

Cover Design & Layout by David Mecham
Printed in the United States of America

*II*

"The respective values of toilet paper and a dollar bill become equal at the precise moment the **18** healthy bran cookies you ate **5** miles ago completely absorb **32** ounces of pre-hike sports drink."

# Contents

# Please Read Before Reading

*Many people are probably wondering: "Why an outhouse book?" The answer to this and other questions is that we did years of exhaustive research, namely, I noticed that I like to read in the cranny. . . and we kind of thought that maybe other people would pay us money for stuff to entertain them when they are bored. We did, however, encounter a problem that could affect the success of this epoch project. Our outhouse doesn't have enough light so I can see the pictures. Just before I was about to widen a couple of cracks to let some light (and wind) in, my neighbor, Don, stopped by and suggested that I just tear out a couple of the unimportant pages in the back of the book and light them on fire. What a great idea! This both improved the lighting and warmed the place up a bit. So, thanks to Don's brilliance, we included a couple of worthless pages here and there for you to use for additional light. . . or any other need you might have.*

*A second major problem came when I re-read this book. After finishing, I was sort of* disgusted with what seemed to be an inordinate amount of whining . . . even for me. I was just about to symbolically feed the whole manuscript to the neighbors' dog, because I hate whiny people when they're not me, and then it hit me like a ton of bricks: What better place to whine than in the outhouse? Many people I know do their best whining on the old "pity pot". Therefore this book, with all of its whining, is sort of symbolic . . . in fact, perfect. So I let it stand.

Now, I know that there are many of you who read in other places; restaurants, libraries, etc. and so, to you I apologize. Just shut up and read.

Oh, and one more thing, since some of you might not be from around here, and therefore might not take what's written in the spirit that it was intended, I thought I might possibly save my writing career by making a few observations. It might be helpful for you to know that the author is a social scientist (which is sort of like a real scientist) who was raised in a rural environment and who now lives in what USED to be a rural environment in the West and who hates watching fields turn into subdivisions, but who spent a few years in-between living in suburban areas (which was the trial of his life). He has done extensive sociological research (which is a little bit like real research only conclusions are drawn without being encumbered by so many actual facts) which has convinced the author that compared to city people - taken as a whole with a few notable exceptions, (Gus Guernsey for instance) - country people have a much better work ethic, are more honest, work harder, are more moral and virtuous, work much harder, deserve to live more, and work a lot harder when compared with city people.

This bias, when combined with a smoldering contempt for city politicians who give the author's hard-earned tax dollars to every self-righteous, arrogant, immoral, wretched, miserable, lazy, self-interested group who gives the politicians money, provided they whine loud enough while they do it, all the while trying to tell the author how

VIII

he should live, has helped to shape the tone of this book.

If this bothers you, you should probably consider only reading chapters 3, 8, 12 and 13, and then skipping to the end. You can read the plugs on the back cover as many times as you want.

If anyone associated with this book has inadvertently used political correctness or showed excessive gender, religious, or race sensitivity, we sincerely apologize.

**Thank you.**

# 1 The Things We Did In The Good Old Days That Today's Wimpy Kids Can't Appreciate

Many of us older folk can remember times when we didn't have it quite so good, soft and easy. I am always receiving entertaining mail from my readers. And after they remind me that I owe them money, they will occasionally offer a reminiscence that they want me to write about in my columns. Some of these reminiscences remind me of my own home...and since misery sometimes makes pretty good reading, I thought I should share some of these with you, my readers. Honestly, I am also doing this partly for the benefit of the rising generation. I'm hoping that my kids might pick it up, maybe thinking it's a Mad Magazine, or something and by reading it develop an appreciation for how tough we had it in the good old days when men were truly men and girls were generally safe only in trees.

Gladys Stern from Dog Wash, Wyoming remembers how her family used to stay warm during the cold winters by stuffing chickens down their clothes. She further explains: "That's where the term, 'colder than 20 chickens' comes from". She remembers that in Wyoming in January it was so cold that people's teeth would often freeze together and a lot of people would starve to death or suffocate.

Maude Hornbill from Horse Flank, Colorado reminisces: "In the summertime, when it got unbearably hot, we were taught to spit on each other out of courtesy."

Scooter Lardner from Pioche, Nevada tells us, "One winter after the crops had all failed. We got so hungry that we filled up on spun glass insulation from the attic and the twinkie wrappers that mom had been saving to make a quilt. One time, on his way home from working in the stone quarry, Dad lucked onto a bunch of skunks. Even though Dad had to eat outside, that was one of the best meals I ever had." He also recalls, "I can remember during one lean time that I had my faithful dog, "Old Blue" out all night hunting toads. I came in with a big sack of them. We were just licking our chops in anticipation of Mom's toad soup, but instead mom gave them all to the neighbors who were worse off than us. All we had to eat that night was dirt and rocks sweetened with transmission fluid. But we learned an important lesson."

Out in Boot Crack, Arizona, Chuck "Bilge Hammer" Banks remembers how, "by putting a dead rat or some other piece of carrion on our heads, we could sometimes coax a hawk or vulture to come after it. When they swooped down, their wings flapping is as close to air conditioning as we got in those days."

Fred Bern in Pyallup, Washington remembers that the key to staying warm in that part of the country was to stay dry, and so they were taught to pour hot tar down their pants. He remembers that this would keep you real warm for a while and when it would harden, you would have a kind of poor man's wet suit.

Dave Bland from Crack Pot, Nevada reminisces, "We were so poor that we couldn't afford nuts in our fruit cakes at Christmas time so Granny would substitute rocks and gravel." He adds, "Every day I milked a couple thousand cows by hand before school. I was so excited when the new shop vacuums came out with a hose attachment...although at first it did take 5 or 6 of us to hold the cow down."

Edsel Wedge from out in Grizzly Cavity, Montana remembers "During the war we couldn't get chocolate...so my brother and I would sneak over to the neighbors ditch. That clay mud sweetened with transmission fluid wasn't so bad as I remember and we were darned glad to have it...but we got in trouble once when we ate all the mud on the lower side of the ditch causing it to break and flood the Brussels sprouts crop."

Lutherene Smedley from Crotchwedge, Texas remembers, "Of course in those days there were no doctors or antibiotics out our way. When we caught a cold, mom would sweat it out of us by putting us in the microwave on a low heat all afternoon."

Homer Duroc from Burley, Idaho recalls, "In our part of Idaho, we had to make all of our own clothes out of materials that were readily available. Of course, we had no money at all. One time, I remember going all summer wearing shorts made from potato peels, stitched together with spaghetti squash."

I, myself have had some of these character-building experiences growing up in Pleasant Grove,

Utah that some of the younger generation could benefit from hearing. I recall when I was a young boy, there were many common things that my mother would make us save for later use. We felt that we couldn't afford to waste anything of value. I remember how she had us save our soiled Kleenex tissues and then she would use them to fill up cracks around the doors and keep out the cold winter wind. She would also have us save egg shells. We could tape them back together and use them for ping-pong balls. Even our toe nail clippings were collected and saved. Mom would show us how to put them inside papier-mache´ to make morocco's, or to sprinkle onto cakes and cookies.

There you have a sampling of contributions from the lives of my readers. This should give you an idea of just what kind of people generally read my column. You young whipper snappers too, if you got all the way through this, now you know how sniveling little snot nosed bug-eyed computer punching wimps would never have survived one week in the old days like your parents did. ◆◆

2

# One Useful Anger
# Management
# Technique

Like many of you, I often find myself
completely surrounded by idiots. People who wait
on me, drive on the same road with me and fix my
broken stuff seem to have the fundamental
intelligence God normally grants a gob of cheese.
The problem is that nowadays, if you call an idiot
an idiot or if you describe him or her publicly in
terms that are descriptive and accurate, bad things
can happen. You can be accused of sexual
harassment, lose your job, be sued out of existence,
shot, maimed or killed. So in order to relieve
tension, when someone does something stupid to
me, while I still call them an entertaining name, I
just keep it quietly to myself. Some days, when it
seems that if idiots could fly, my place would be an

airport, I become so entertained with my own thoughts that I break out laughing...causing some people to occasionally mistake me for the idiot in question.

Recently, I dropped by the office to see my younger brother, right after having stood in line for half an hour while a person was ignoring me at the post office, just following having been run off the road by a blind, deaf, terminally common-sensed disadvantaged driver, after having witnessed one of the most poorly officiated basketball games ever played. I was inspired.

I was chuckling to myself thinking that I had raised this mental name-calling skill to new levels when it happened. My brother gave me a poor, well-circulated office copy of a list of politically correct names to call people who are not too bright. I was not only bummed because someone came up with some better ones than I did, but I nearly choked to death on my gum from laughing so hard.

So, since I recommend this private name calling technique as a form of anger management, sometimes to be used in place of automatic weapons and gang violence, I would like to share this combined list (It includes some of the names that I came up with added to some of the best terms from the list circulating around my brother's office) with you, my readers. Like me, some of you may have heard a few of these already...some might hear them every day...regularly. And by the way, for those of you who worry about it, you will also find that a few are politically correct, so you can feel free to use them in front of your kids and in public.

# Some politically correct ways to tell someone or something that he, she, or it is an idiot, jerk, dork, dweebe, imbecile, or moron

## He, she or it:

Has an IQ of 2, but it takes 3 to grunt

◆

Ate too many square meters of
lead-based house paint

◆

Is dumber than a box of hair

◆

Normally can finish the maze just a few hours
behind the rats

◆

Is an experiment in artificial intelligence

◆

Wouldn't appear to be quite so stupid if you could

9

surround him with invertebrates

Is missing a few buttons on her remote control

Let the local veterinary school try one too many
experimental brain surgeries

Forgot to pay her brain bill

Is operating with his head on the "NUMB" setting

Doesn't know much but leads the
league in nostril hair

Doesn't have all his dogs on a leash

◆

Is as smart as bait

◆

Fell out of the stupid tree and hit every
branch on the way down

◆

Couldn't pour water out of a boot with
instructions on the heel

◆

Is all foam, no beer

◆

Seems smart enough unless you compare

him to your appendix

Is surfing in Nebraska

Is about as bright as a burp

Seems to have been attacked by a battalion of
Klingons with their phasers set on "stun"

Is a few fries short of a happy meal

## His, Her, or Its:

Receiver is off the hook

Bunji cord was a foot too long

Belt doesn't go through all the loops

Antenna doesn't pick up all the channels

Slinky's kinked

Gold fish are flopping all over the table

Elevator doesn't go all the way to the top floor

◆

Intellect is rivaled only by garden tools

◆

Antennae doesn't pick up all the channels

# And:

The wheel's spinning but the hamster's dead

◆

On the freeway of life, his mind is a pothole

◆

If she had another brain it would be lonely

◆

The lights are on but nobody's home

◆

When compared to Gilligan, she doesn't
seem too bright

◆

In the game yesterday, he let them use his
brain for second base.

◆

Warning:  Objects in mirror are dumber
than they appear

◆

If brains were acne he couldn't worry a
teenage girl

◆

Trading brains with a marmoset would be an
improvement

So there you go.  I give you permission to try these on anyone who annoys you with their stupidity...even if you only mumble the terms to yourself.  And, if you should ever come up with any new zingers of your own, please share them with me.  ◆◆

```
(Emergency Square)
```

# 3

## Bad Farming Ideas

People in agriculture are among the most helpful in the world. Most ranchers and farmers I know are willing to share their experiences with their neighbors to help them avoid repeating expensive mistakes. I have been the recipient of the generosity of many of my neighbors who have offered suggestions. While I know that their intent was to be helpful, I must admit that I have become more cautious over the years because, quite frankly, some of their suggestions didn't work. Since some of you may also look and act like the type of person who could use lots of suggestions, I think that it's only proper that I pass my experience on to you. Maybe you can avoid some of the mistakes that I have made when I followed the suggestions of my neighbors.

I should note that I just recently started keeping track of who gave which suggestion. I didn't used to write down the name of the person who gave me the tip and so I can't always remember who it was...and liability has been tough to establish. Even so, I suggest that you listen to experience. Don't try the following things; and don't ever say I didn't warn you.

## Wayne's bad farming ideas which we suggest you never try:

1. Using a bloated cow as a family room sofa...or giant whoopee cushion.

2. Developing a breed of rabbits big enough to pull a plow.

3. Starting a commercial toad operation.

4. Raising skunks for their hides.

5. Trying to resuscitate a 1978 Dodge pickup by exhaling into the tailpipe while the key is on and the motor running.

6. Using the marijuana crop planted in-between your corn rows as collateral for a loan to

pay your taxes.

7. Using nuclear waste on your corn field as a soil builder, even if the driver who's truck tipped over let you keep it for free out of gratitude because you let him use your equipment to clean up the mess.

8. In order to pacify animal rights activists, using pink hair ribbons to mark your cattle in place of branding.

9. Having the junior high shop class maintain your equipment to save money and contribute to the community.

10. Using an acetylene torch to burn the cat fur out of your tractor treads.

11. Turning hundreds of chickens loose to roam your wheat fields in order to get the benefit of natural organic fertilizer.

12. Using energy from burning haystacks to operate your mint still.

13. Using your witching sticks to search for the spark plugs in your diesel tractor.

14. Borrowing against the money from

future tax cuts promised by politicians during this year's election campaign.

15. Feeding your livestock or pets on hospital surgical waste without first picking out the syringes.

16. Using herbicide, pesticide and genocide packages to grind up for use as cellulose attic insulation.

17. Hooking jumper cables to the battery of your pace-maker to jump start your tractor.

18. Pouring your life savings into a commercial aphid farm.

19. Trying to run your equipment on ethanol made from distilled sugar-coating from campaign promises.

20. Using your come-along to straighten out your kids' crooked teeth.

21. Trying to pull your John Deere tractor which is stuck up to its axle's out in the field with your neighbor's daughter's Geo Metro.

22. Trying to reduce the number of times that you have to clean out the dairy by designing a

loin cloth/diaper for the cows' backsides.

23.  Creating new markets for your crops by inventing new products and tasty dishes such as:  A new line of agricultural perfumes, alfalfa-flavored toothpaste, Hamburger Helper made from ground corn silage.

24.  Trying to save money by-passing a few steps in the sugar beet food production process encouraging people to pour nitrogen phosphate fertilizer granules directly onto their cereal.  ◆◆

```
(Emergency Square)
```

# 4
# New Plant Varieties

This week I got my first bunch of plants and seeds back from the seed catalogues. One of our favorite annual family rituals is reading them and looking at the bright, colorful pictures of all of the new varieties of trees, bushes, fruits and vegetables. This year, for example, we are planting a "pluot" tree for the first time, (a pluot being 75% plum and 25% apricot). In the past we've tried cold hardy kiwis, giant pumpkins, and a giant dog, cat, and aphid-eating praying mantis.

I've been fascinated for years with this tedious process of genetic trial and error which ultimately yields a new plant species useful to man. But because I know that we consumers only hear of the successes, never the failures, I have often wondered about the new types of plants which, for some reason or another never made it into broad public acceptance.  Because this is an area of particular interest to me, I took it upon myself to do some research on the topic and, thanks to Ervin Dorenbosch of the local nursery, I got some information about new plant varieties which never made the big time or still have some problems to work out.

For example, they have been working for a few years on improving the taste of common garden beets by cross-pollinating them with plums. The product ultimately was an improvement, but never gained wide acceptance because of marketing snags.  Both the variety which was 75% beet and 25% plum and the one that was the opposite simply never flew out the doors of the nurseries in market tests.  It seems as though no one would buy a "Bum" or a "Peet".

Another marketing failure occurred when botanists determined to get rid of the smell and watery eyes caused by onions by crossing them with a grape.  The problem then was that no one wanted to buy a "Grunion" and they couldn't give away a "oRape".

A little known experiment was conducted a while back that also wound up having marketing problems when scientists found a use for some of President Clinton's excess body fluids that were beginning to cause storage problems at so many crime labs around the country. To raise money for the Democratic National Committee, they sold some of them to science. Scientists figured that they could use some of the DNA to try to cross-pollinate celery and other vegetables thereby hoping to improve it. The result was an interesting vegetable which miraculously would taste like whatever you wanted it to at the time. The problem with it was that it had no fiber whatever.

Another failure occurred when they crossed a banana with a skunk and called it Bunk. It tasted like chicken but no one would buy it either.

In an attempt to develop a type of bean which wouldn't cause gas, scientists crossed common kidney beans with cheese. This caused the first tragic accident when one of the taste testers got so plugged up that the poor guy who ate it exploded in the lab and completely disappeared. The rumors circulating around plant nurseries is that they blamed it on alien abduction.

Even I have gotten into the act trying to develop new species of useful plants. For the last few years I have been consistently able to grow a tomato which has a trendy, large, brown spot on the bottom. The pigs love it! I've also developed a strain of house plants for people like me with a green thumb, that you never have to water. Left completely on their own, in time, they grow to an attractive light brown color and look a little like dried flower arrangements. ◆◆

# 5

## Pet Peeves

A short time ago, while planning one of my columns, I asked my readers to send me some of their pet peeves. Never have I received such a response to anything I've written. I was overwhelmed. In fact, my readers are probably the biggest bunch of whiners I have ever met. Since usually what goes around comes around, and since sometimes it can be beneficial to know exactly how to subtly push someone else's buttons, I thought it would be a good idea to publish a few of these pet peeves. By so doing, I can share some of the anxiety I feel knowing the kind of people who are allowed to walk the streets unrestrained...and we might give law enforcement officials and city planners a jump on planning construction for new facilities. The following is a partial list of things that people hate:

Erma in Formaldehyde, Wyoming said she hates it "When the goat licks your face and you're not expecting it and so your mouth's open. She also hates stepping in a wet cow pie with bare feet.

Bill Mobley from Gunnison, Colorado hates it when you pour Roquefort dressing into your salad, dig in, and one of the lumps turns out to be a cockroach.

Melba Doernbosch of Whiskey Springs, Nevada hates getting her cat get caught in the snow blower.

Rick Farrer from Royal City, Washington says that his pet peeve is when the guy who's beating you up gets hold of your nose hairs.

Douglas Anderton of Wilcox, Arizona hates constantly finding bits of toilet paper in his refried beans.

Farley Hemlock from Anthrax, Colorado hates it when your appendix ruptures and you don't have anything to remove it with except a butter knife with raspberry jam on it and a vacuum cleaner.

Although I've been told that it's bad journalism to do so, I am going to print some of the responses that came in anonymously. For some reason, people refused to sign their names to these pet peeves, but it looks to me like they can still be useful. Some of my readers, I'm sure will relate to the following:

"I hate it when, while hanging from a 20 story window sill, a pigeon poops on your forehead...

...When you're so preoccupied trying to get into your locked car while the motor's running with the keys in it that you don't even notice when some jerk steals your hubcaps...

...Pouring a big glass of lemonade and it turns out to be liquid plumber...

...Mistaking analgesic for sunscreen...

...While pulling out a tree stump. getting the chain accidentally wrapped around your neck just when you yell "GO" to the tractor driver...

...Being dragged behind your horse when he decides to swim a river...

...Running out of Sears Catalogue pages in the

outhouse and being forced to use your power
sander...

...Biting into an apple and seeing half-a-worm...

...Sleeping in the barn and waking up to find that
chickens have been perching above you...

...Blowing your nose and having the stuff fill up
your bottom lip...

...Seeing a 72 year old 360 pound woman...or man
in a string bikini...

...Getting your tongue tangled up in
your chain saw...

Finally, I should mention that rancher,
Melvin Conjugal from Goiter, Oregon insists that
his pet peeve is having a supposedly well-informed
prominent talk show host connect eating beef with
slow torture while being pecked to death by tweety
birds and then eaten by squirrels.

Twila Conjugal from nearby Paregoric
Oregon says that she hates it when a prominent talk
show host draws a connection between eating beef
and having the few children in the world who
didn't self-abort mutate into reptiles.

Lewis Conjugal also from Goiter says that he would hate it every time that a prominent talk show host were to choke on her tofu, inhale one of the pages from her fitness book and strangle in her microphone chord and die...and he's not bitter.

So there they are. People sort of like you and their pet peeves. Enjoy them, and if you're ever a talk show host, be sure and use caution when discussing topics which might adversely affect people's livelihoods. ◆◆

```
(Emergency Square)
```

# Western Wisdom

Whenever you get tired of viewing the lead-dog's
backside, you can always close your eyes
and visualize a cheeseburger.

It's better to aim your spear at the moon and hit
only a rock than to toss your pipe bomb
at a cat and hit your uncle Mel's Winnebago.

A frost-covered outhouse seat
yields few splinters.

◆

If you're gonna be a turd, go lay in the yard.

◆

Never blow-dry a frog; they don't have much hair

and it makes them smaller.

People who live in glass houses often have to shower in the dark and get real hot in the summer time.

An old geezer is like an old tire; bald in most spots, with a bulge here and there; but if you patch the holes and pump them both full of air, one of them makes a pretty good flotation device.

He who uses the last square will one day himself be caught sitting with an empty roll.

You won't get much milk from a cow who has a rubber band around her udders.

People who pick their scabs shouldn't swim in contaminated water.

A snake could jump higher if only it had legs.

If you insist on trying to milk a bull, at least it's better if it's a small one.

A short temper is better than a long bunji chord.

Girls who have no teeth have to work
a little harder to get asked out to dinner.

If you find that you keep landing face first in
buffalo chips, you will be less disgusted if you keep
your mouth shut.

Spiders don't scamper so fast after your son pulls
their legs off.

```
(Emergency Square)
```

# 7 A Collection of Pioneer Remedies You May Want to Try... On Someone Else

**Itchy Insect Bites:**

Melba Toad of Littleton, Colorado writes, "My Grandma Maude had a couple of terrific ways to make pesky mosquito bites stop itching. The first way is to rub the affected area briskly with a cheese grater and then pour a little bit of Italian Dressing on the affected area. If that doesn't work, a sure way is to put a Jalapeno Pepper in each nostril or have someone stomp on your toe."

**For Gas, Constipation, Hiccoughs, Appendicitis, or Hepatitis "B"**

Al Burger of Pioche, Nevada shares the following: "Take orally 12 cups of grated rutabaga,

3 boiled eggs (include the shells), and 1-quart water with 1 cup of baking soda mixed in (you can also substitute 24 Alka Seltzer tablets."

*Al also insists that this potion, if taken regularly can also reduce your chances of osteoporosis in later years.

## Appetite Suppressant and Weight Loss

A sure-fire low cost weight-loss, appetite suppressant was submitted to us by Flora Bunderson of Moose Doot, Montana. She advises: Much cheaper and probably healthier than drugs is to simply lift up the septic tank cover and take a deep breath just before each meal...or if you don't yet have indoor plumbing or for some other reason don't have a septic tank, you can get a similar effect by turning the compost pile."

Irvene Twitchell from Paragonah, Utah suggests that to suppress your appetite, go for a ride in the car with a goat, preferably male...or during the political season, tape political commercials throughout the next couple of years, replay some before each meal. This will definitely kill your appetite."

Her husband, Earl, says it works just as good for him to kill his appetite to just eat a candy bar before each meal.

## Infections

Whenever my grandma, who once was this region's country mid-wife, used to deliver babies or perform open heart surgery, in order to limit infections, she used the pioneer remedy of applying a poultice to the incision made up of hydrogenated vegetable oil, defatted wheat germ, and rubbing alcohol...or hydrogen peroxide.

## Radiation Sickness

For radiation sickness, Ethyl Donwinder of St. George, UT says that her family used to put a leach on the scabs. "We're not too sure whether or not they did any good, but at least someone was getting some good out of those sores." When she would catch her kids eating lead-based paint, she knew right away that the radiation was sapping vital nutrients from her kids bodies. To remedy it she would mix a little sand into the frosting on cupcakes and cookies. Many down winders could save money reading by the glow of each other. ◆◆

# 8

# Rookie Ranchers; Follow This Advice On Fencing

If you happen to be a novice rancher, you have no doubt begun to observe the wide variety of fences that your neighbors have erected. If you're planning to fence your new spread, at this moment you could be completely overwhelmed with all of the choices that exist. Being neighborly neighbors, we want to help make your transition from city to country...and back again as smooth as possible. Therefore, we have compiled this pile of information to help make your fencing decisions easier.

At this very moment, you could be staring at the old fence that exists on the place you just bought and contemplating spending the big bucks to have city contractors put in an artificial-looking synthetic, and terribly expensive petroleum-derived imitation white pole fence.

Hold your horses. You might be about to destroy an extremely useful and historic piece of fencing in favor of something which often won't keep anything in or out after having been transmorphed into some breathtaking and stunning works of art each spring when the neighbors on the other side of the fence burn their weeds. The fence you already own is no less than an exquisite type we call the "Chardonnay" fence. It gets this name from being aged to perfection. The best ones were erected during the Truman administration. The thing that sets a premium Chardonnay apart from other fences is the character in the form of decaying wood, soft spots and sagging barbed wire.

Don't jump to conclusions thinking that these soft spots need to be fixed. The truth is that veteran ranchers plan and cultivate these spots in order to stimulate their cows and horses to reach their full intellectual potential by giving them constant reinforcement, encouraging them that they can succeed in getting out...if they persist. Good Chardonnays have an excellent rate of retention, often holding up to 90% of your standard cows and horses as much as 90% of the time. This classic fence could be just what you need...unless you have the misfortune of owning a cow like Blackie.

If you've tried it for a while and your Chardonnay just isn't working to your satisfaction, and you are saddled with an average rural persons' budget, (commonly known as "no budget") you might want to try the second type of fence that is popular with ranching professionals. We call this the Econo-fence. It's main advantages are it's cost, and it's unique aesthetic art value. Also, if it's done right it will give some of your troublesome critters a new look and maybe slow their escapes down...for a while at least.

As we mentioned earlier, the overriding objective of this fence is to avoid spending money. True professionals can build a mile of Econo-fence on less than a dollar. In order to build a good one, you must be a good scavenger. You will need to develop a sharp eye as you hunt around the yard and surrounding areas for practical and artistic items that can be used, that don't appear to belong to anyone with a bad attitude. These can be materials that you actually own yourself or which are owned by the government or other large utility, or who will never miss them. There is a wide range of fencing materials that will work in place of expensive fence posts and barbed wire. To name just a few, consider old cars, bed posts, outhouses, common road signs that have been discarded by the high way department, TV antennas, parts of large, deceased animals, hub caps, formerly legal but currently illegal herbicide containers in varying sizes and colors, rusty bicycles and tractor parts.

There are really no standard instructions on

how to build a fence from this type of material. You just connect the stuff you found together as best you can and turn your livestock in, hoping for the best. This fence will keep many of your cows and horses in...sometimes for hours at a time, unless you have the misfortune of owning a troublesome cow like Blackie.

After having owned livestock for a while, you need to watch that you don't undergo a personality trans-mutation. This sometimes happens from the frustration of trying to keep critters in without success and having had valuable herbal assets eaten and trampled, and possibly even being the party of a law suit for damage to the cars that ran into Blackie when he was inspecting the high way. Some ranchers find that they have become so demented that they no longer care about the safety or comfort of the animals that they once loved. Every once in a while you will see some frustrated rancher stretching electrical wire and insulated poles around the field, bypassing the 12-volt battery and stringing connecting cables directly to the high-voltage transmission wires running near the property. He does this in the hopes of either teaching Blackie a lesson that he will never forget, or else saving the cost of butchering the animal by barbecuing it right there on the wire.

We don't recommend that you use this type of fencing. But since we understand how easy it is to become upset with your critters, we want you to know that if you choose to go this route, find some way other than sticking your tongue on the wire or relieving yourself on it to test whether or not it's hot...And, be sure to scrape the barbecue off the fence using something that is a poor conductor of electricity. ◆◆

```
(Emergency Square)
```

# 9 Impressing City Women

One of my good friends, Spud, has managed to stay single for over 4 decades. Some of the rest of my buddies who don't know the true situation are pretty impressed, some are even envious. Deep down inside, I know that in the worst way, Spud would like to have a bride. In some ways, he would be a fine catch too...for the right girl. His problem is that during the critical getting acquainted stage, in ways that he doesn't fully understand, he keeps inadvertently sabotaging his own efforts.

The problem now is that, he's pretty much blown it with all of the girls around here to the point that he can hardly get a date. Recently, I suggested that it would be a good idea if he expanded his dating horizons to include a few cultured city girls. This was a perfectly terrifying thought to him. So, in the spirit of true friendship, I offer these tips to my buddy Spud. And since there are probably a good many more "Spuds" out there in other parts of the country, some of whom can read, I thought it would be a good idea to publish these helps.

## The following will not impress city women:

1. Going straight to a church social without a shower after work...especially if you work at the organic fertilizer plant

2. Wearing the toupee you made yourself from the pheasant you shot

3. Polishing your teeth with your ear wax

4. When your nose starts to bleed because the Ferris wheel ride got too high, leaving the hankie stuffed up there while you go dancing

5. Yodeling while you sing "Amazing Grace" at your Aunt Mildred's funeral

6. Taking your city date out for a special evening and letting her shoot the steer at the slaughter house

7. Describing your hemorrhoid transplant surgery in graphic detail

8. Bragging about running over a record 9 cats in one night

9. Inviting her to come over for a fun night of helping you clean and cut up the deer that you shot

10. Curling and waxing your nose hairs

11. Showing off you how far you can spit

12. Borrowing one of her hair pins to clean out your teeth after dinner

13. Planting a big smooch on her lips right after she watches you give a sloppy kiss to your pet pig, Elton

14. Having the foresight to wear your black rubber boots and "Dickeys" coveralls to dinner at a posh Italian restaurant in case you get a chance to stop and help pull people out of the snow with your tractor

There, all you spuds out there. Maybe this might help you get a second date with those city girls. ◆◆

# 10

# Is Your Glass Half Empty, Half Full... or Being Recycled?

Among other deep philosophical concepts, my dad taught me that happiness is a state of mind. While it's true that my dad doesn't watch Oprah Winfrey or never had to try to start a business with Bill Clinton as president, and did most of his banking while talking to actual people instead of machines, which probably made it easier for him to have a healthy perspective, still, I believe it's true that a person's happiness is determined in large part by how one looks at the daily small problems like getting your hair tangled around the Weed Eater, trying to be patient while your kids chase down the guy who parked his pickup on your feet,...or having someone bump your elbow causing you to staple one of your nostrils shut with your staple gun. The fact is that set-backs and bummers are a major part of everyone's life. I have had more than my share lately for some reason, so I have been working hard on my attitude by practicing my healthy perspective.

I suspect that there may be some of my readers who have a high number of irritations, and since they most likely got raised by somebody besides my dad, I consider it my duty to share some of the Allred ways of looking at things. Therefore, no matter how wretched and miserable your real life is, there are always a few things like these that you could be happy about. When you get to thinking that your life is miserable, take a minute and consider this:

When you woke up this morning you probably
were not buried under a ton of concrete.

Although your dog is lying along side the road in
front of your house, the neighbors' cat is also
decomposing across the street.

Even if some day the country should be
overrun by Iraqi armies and bombed by nuclear
weapons, decades later you could still find
hot dogs and twinkies in the dump which you can
eat to survive because they won't decompose
for a century or more since their half-life

is longer than the nuclear fallout.

◆

Although you have gained 50 unwanted pounds,
now you are able to stay warmer
without extra clothes.

◆

Even after your septic tank backed up and flooded
your house with 8 inches of rancid fecal matter,
after you shovel it outside, your lawn
will be greener.

◆

The burglars who stole your jewelry, TV, computer,
money, and small appliances some how missed the
salami in the fridge.

◆

The fact that your car wouldn't start has probably
kept you from getting another speeding ticket.

◆

It's sad that you returned from town to find all of
your fish belly up in their tank, but hey, now you
have something inexpensive and different to put
into your Jell-O mold.

◆

If only dorks and geeks will ever ask you out, don't
feel bad. Geeks are one of the few classes of
human beings who will still pay for the date...and
dorks can help you with your home work.

After the complete destruction of the Brazilian rain forest, as all of the starving refugees stream north, they will overrun Belize and Guatemala long before they ever get to you.

So they build a toxic waste incinerator next door to you, there has to be a big market someplace for glow-in-the-dark potatoes.

Termites are probably not marching out of your nose and ears

You are not a squid

You were most likely not born with portions of your butt growing out of your face

You were never married to Henry the VIII

The typical way that you derive your nutrition is not from converting fecal matter into nitrogen

You are not still on the Titanic or the Hindenberg

Pollen grains and dust mites don't grow to be as big as your head

There, now I've got you started, you can begin working on viewing your own problems from the "half full" perspective. Who knows, maybe we can reduce your Prosac bill for a few years. ◆◆

(Emergency Square)

# A True Pioneer Story. . . Sort Of

It's 1997. Do you know where your ancestors are? If they were just a little less dead, they would probably be out causing all kinds of trouble right now.

Did you know that in 1882, there were 27 workers from China living out West in Roslyn, Washington, who, thanks to your delinquent ancestors, suddenly woke up dead one morning? These Chinese, along with all Blacks and others, were at the time legally excluded from many activities in the state of Washington and the community of Roslyn -- such as owning property, voting, choosing not to be shot or lynched, and breathing.

To those of us with late 20th-century social

consciences, this obvious disregard for human rights is a little hard to comprehend; but your ancestors understood perfectly. There were many reasons why people of the 19th century felt that they should not be hospitable toward these incoming foreigners.

For starters, between the 1870s and the 1920s it was common practice to give intelligence tests to many arriving immigrants. The new immigrants usually didn't do so well on them. Most new comers were so dense that they couldn't understand plain English. They couldn't even answer the simplest questions about Charles Lindbergh, quantum physics, Michael Jackson, or Ty Cobb. And, though it's hard for some of us today to imagine such illiteracy, most had difficulty identifying and understanding many popular Shakespearean phrases such as "A penny saved is a penny earned" or "the Opera ain't over till the fat lady sings." This proved conclusively to people of the time that these people were "feeble minded".

Other reasons why your ancestors hated immigrants, especially the Chinese, included the fear of billions of people overwhelming America if they let them all move in freely, plus the fact that they would work for much less than usual, and they thought they were very, very weird.

But back to our story...On a hot summers night in 1882, in the town of Roslyn, Washington, a group of men dressed like local Indians (who 20 years earlier had inadvertently been completely killed off in the area) invaded the Chinese camp on the outskirts of town and systematically executed the Chinese workers there. The Chinese immigrants were all killed except one. A total of 27 Chinese men were butchered. I emphasize this number because details about the massacre along with information as to the reason why one lone survivor was spared, has since passed on with the perpetrators. Then contemporary Washingtonians let the incident die (no pun intended) with little or no news coverage and a hasty investigation.

To those of us living in the 1990s, this too is hard to understand. Something as gory and sensational as the murder of 27 people should have been plastered over every television screen in every log cabin in America for months. It would have been an event as big as the Super bowl, Oprah's great grandmother's weight, or President Taft's underwear. If this happened now days we would be hearing about it until we were all seeing massacred Chinese workers in our dreams.

I can think of only 3 possible reasons why people in the late 1800s didn't get caught up in this event like they should have. Either there were too many more important massacres going on at the same time and this one just couldn't generate the interest, or the people who did it had grown up in disadvantaged environments entitling them to our understanding and a different set of legal expectations, or the people who were guilty supervised a series of gruesome and unfortunate accidents which happened to anyone who showed any interest in the deaths, making witnesses reluctant to talk about it. We modern folk are left only to wonder which of these explanations is the right one.

After 15 exhaustive minutes of investigation, officials concluded that the killers must have indeed been those rascals, the non-existent Indians, and since they had already been dead for 20 years and would therefore be difficult to catch for questioning, they had better just close the books on this one.

No, I am not advocating opening the files again. I have coached school basketball against Cle Elum and Roslyn. One Salman Rushdie in the world is enough. There would be no point anyway because now, thanks to Ralph Nadar, Phil Donahue, the ACLU, and Geraldo, and the fact that your misguided but bigoted relatives are dead, we all speak in reverent tones about minority groups: American soccer players, people who like cats, those who voted for Richard Nixon, people who own a successful small business, and married people living together. We don't need to worry about bigotry anymore.

Now days, not only can we live in any state that we choose regardless of our ethnicity, but if we threaten the right people, we can get any government job we want, (unless we happen to have the misfortune of being male, white, or from a wealthy family). We can become president of any company in America, (unless we happen to be black, brown, red, or female). And, we can be a tourist anywhere we want (just so it's not in a big city, and we don't look foreign or wealthy).

It's a good thing that those bigoted ancestors of ours have moved on to their just rewards. We can only hope that the culprits of the 27 murders of Chinese, whoever and wherever they are, are getting their due.

Meanwhile, I'll just leave those skeletons about your ancestors in your closets. It will be a secret just between me and you and the other people who read this column. And we can just go on being thankful that no one around here has to worry any more about being limited in their upward mobility by their race or gender or perversion. ◆◆

# 12 Creative Ways Of Cleaning Up The World

The world is shrinking. Amazing advances in telecommunications make it possible at a moment's notice, for the entire world to be aware of the type of underwear our president wears. It's possible, because of supersonic transport, to travel to any part of the globe in only a day...even faster if you go by fax. All of the low places in the world are being filled up with garbage and toxic waste and dead spotted owls.

We country people want to do our part to help make the world a cleaner place. Since we would go to jail if we sewed all Rap singers' mouths' shut, or used Madonna, and dead politicians to compost our potato field, or sent Dennis Rodman to outer Mongolia where he would feel more at home, we have to resort to rural farmer type ingenuity to reduce our waste and garbage.

Recently, right after our team got beat in the football playoffs, while we were pretty loose and thinking creatively, me and my buddies decided to put our heads together and come up with some things that we could do to set an environmental example for the rest of the country. Here is what we came up with. And I hereby challenge all the rest of you to wipe the smirks off from your faces and follow our fine example and create your own list of things you can do to clean up the environment. Then next year, if we feel like it, we can DO some of them...I think. Well, anyway, here's our list.

1. We committed to lighting all of our campfires with non-leaded gasoline.

2. In an effort to conserve water, we committed to bathing only once a week, to eating with our fingers or toad stabber so that there aren't so many dishes to wash, and to taking the clothes from the hamper and wearing them a couple more weeks before we put them in the washing machine.

3. We are going to go way beyond the simple planting of a tree to help clean the air. We hereby commit to planting an entire field of potatoes or alfalfa. This will both clean the air and fertilize the ground at the same time feeding a few starving folks.

4. In order to have more fuel efficient

equipment and pickups, We committed to put those annoying catalytic converters and smog equipment back on the trucks and vehicles we took it off from...if we can find it.

5. In order to save the lives of trees, my entire family is working to recycle paper, especially toilet paper. For example, my daughter, Kelsey, was a mummy for Halloween. Her costume was 95% toilet paper which was wrapped around her about a hundred times. We felt that this paper was still perfectly good, except where she spilled pop on it. And so we put it into a plastic bucket and set it next to the commode for people to use instead of new paper. It worked great too if you just take a little time to straighten it out...and pick out the pieces of duct tape which clog up the plumbing. Also, I should mention that we have tried to clean the toilet paper out of the tallest parts of our trees, some of which has been there for up to 6 or 7 toilet paperings. All of this goes into a big 5-gallon bucket next to the commode for use and re-use by our family and guests, if we ever have any.

6. Furthermore, we all committed to the support of endangered species, especially those like heterosexual couples who stay together until they die, honest working men and women who don't expect the government to solve all of their problems for them, and honest, hard-working public servants. For this entire year, whenever I stumble across one of these, we hereby promise not

to shoot them.

    7. And finally, in order to take a giant stride toward cleaning up the environment, we vowed to not patronize trashy movies or TV shows...in fact, if we could find somewhere else to watch the football games, we might decide to get rid of the TV altogether.

    While I am certain that there are other things that we could have written down, if we think about doing these things, we will be doing at least as much as most other people to clean up our environment and make this world a better place.

# More Ways to Not Impress City Women:

Tucking your pants into your boots to show off
your new "Baby Spotted Owl-Skinned" boots

◆

Showing off your manhood by performing your
trick of snorking a whole glass of root beer and
then holding your nose
while you blow it all out your ears

◆

Letting her ride into town in the back

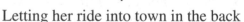

of your new Dodge pickup

Eating with both hands so you can
get done faster

Allowing her to experience the miracle of life by
pulling with both hands on the calf
that's having a hard time being born

Clipping off a chunk of her hair with your sheep
shears just to tease her a little

Letting her hold your cup of "Chew Juice"
during the movie

Parking in your pickup truck with the windows
down at the sulfur springs

Planning a date of hoeing spuds or sugar beets

Introducing her to your cousin, Floyd

Admitting that those other people are your
relatives too

# 13 Science Proves That Country Life is Better Than City... Sort Of

Since earliest times most people who have had a choice would rather live in the country than the city. Normal, non-sociopathic humans seem to be born with intuition that tells them life is nicer out in the wide-open spaces. Recently, scientific evidence has been produced to show that there is good reason for these feelings. Here at my high-tech living room laboratory, we have been analyzing some of these studies. These include apparently thorough research including vertical, horizontal, and bi-lateral studies, which seem to us to prove what you and I have known all along; that country people live longer and healthier, are probably smarter and are definitely better looking than city people. We would like to cite just a few examples of the latest research in support of these notions:

Methane gas, long a favorite topic of country dinner conversations, has recently been in tree-hugger-related city news. Incredibly, it has taken city scientists hundreds of years to figure out that cows are big producers of methane gas. We wonder what caused the light bulb to go off just now. With this startling revelation, environmentally conscious city people worry that bovine methane-rich flatulations are destroying our atmosphere. I don't want to be one to criticize modern city-science, but most country people were shocked to learn that city people assumed that humans are the only species who release gas and even more amazed to know that it hadn't occurred to city people that methane gas emitted by the millions of city humans was harder on the atmosphere than the methane emitted by cows. We think that we would like to see a study done that compares the volume of methane gas produced by cows to the volume produced by city people. This just could reveal that the reason why city people are so slow to figure out obvious scientific facts is that their brains are damaged by methane gas produced by these millions of human city dwellers.

A second study that we looked at for a long time, but couldn't make sense out of used big words that we didn't know and we think they just made them up. On top of that, what little we could understand from it was that some of these same non-country scientists have taken to dissecting people's brains trying to figure out what makes people tick. We worry about the future of city life. It takes a dangerously trusting person to allow somebody to probe around in their brain just to satisfy their curiosity. Since I never met a country person who was actually stupid enough to let someone do this, I realized that the results of the research must skewed by the fact that they are using exclusively city brains! What better scientific proof, nay, prima-facie evidence could there be of the superiority of country intelligence. (Note that this is all in spite of all the cow-produced methane gas that we're breathing which these brain damaged city people are worrying about.)

Third, we cite as scientific proof of the superiority of country living the old guys sitting down town on the bench in front of the department store. City people don't have geezers sitting down town on their benches. Our codgers are very very old, how old, we don't know, but we do know they are at least as old as many forms of common dirt. On the other hand, I defy you to find old CITY people sitting down town on city park benches. You can't do it! The closest thing we've been able to find are bag/shopping-cart persons. The problem with making comparisons between bag persons and country bench-sitting codgers is that while the city geezers look like they're in their 80's, there is really no way to tell. Their kids and grand kids aren't around to verify their ages. My scientific conclusion is that in fact they just look like old people, but they're really only around 20 or so (and they have been exposed to almost no country cow induced methane gas.). It's probably the drugs.

In the absence of hard scientific research on the subject, we propose 3 possible reasons why city fogies don't sit downtown on park benches:

1. There are no old city people which supports our hypothesis on the superiority of country living.

2. Anything that stayed in one place in the city for more than just a few minutes got shot or spray-painted.

3. They never have become acquainted with any of their neighbors, so they don't have any friends to go downtown and talk to.

The final fact that I would like to cite as proof that country life is better than city life is that country kids don't de-evolve. If you have ever ventured into the city downtown in the past couple of decades you were no doubt shocked to see little mutated evidences of Darwin's evolutionary theories running (or rather shuffling and dragging their sagging pants) all over the place. Some have tattoos of naked mythological creatures carved over 90% of their bodies. Some are in the middle of national ugly hair cut contests. Some have everything from chicken bones to Hoola Hoops and broken beer bottles poked into and through holes they have made through their various protruding and often highly sensitive body parts. On the contrary, country kids just look like kids. We have to assume that it's the methane gas.

So there you have it. Hard scientific proof that life in the country is better than life in the city. But don't spread this data around. Otherwise, we might have millions of them moving out here bringing their human induced methane gas to damage our country atmosphere. ◆◆

```
(Emergency Square)
```

# 14

# Fun With Vegetarians

Being an avid follower of new trends, recently I have noticed that everyone is claiming to be going vegetarian. Never wanting to be accused of not being trendy, I got to the point where I knew that I had to try it too...at least for a few hours. My experiment would have lasted longer too if not for the problem of I got to thinking: Adolph, my sister's cat, would have no problem at all eating me if I were dead. In fact, if I were dead, probably the only reason why he wouldn't eat me would be because he was holding out for scrambled eggs with shrimp bits in it, or something even better, certainly not because he had any ethical qualms.

Now, I don't mean to suggest that at this point and in this frame of mind that I would ever consider eating Adolph, but I do want to point out what to me appears to be the most obvious flaw in the cute little animal vegetarian argument. Namely, out there in the real dog eat dog world (no pun intended), if they ever had the chance, any one of these cute little animals wouldn't lift a claw to help a human in our time of need. In fact, they wouldn't ever even think twice of sinking their teeth into our prime rib.

After contemplating these facts for a while, and at the same time getting a little hungry for a bacon cheese burger, like a dog to it's vomit, instead of becoming a permanent vegetarian, I decided to go back to living and eating the way I had before. I went back to using vegetarians like I always had, purely for entertainment. Over the years, I've made a practice of going to eating establishments and, as I'm eating my prime rib or hamburger, I make my eyes real big and chew with my mouth open all the while making imitation dying animal noises between bites. Then I can observe the reaction of the people who I presume to be vegetarians in the place, those who are eating their tofu burgers. If you haven't already become a complete vegetarian, I recommend that you try this too. It can be fun. ◆◆

children about...the "s" word.

    At our place it works like this: Every year
we take all of the kids to the annual cattle round up
at Uncle Wiley's ranch. I thank my good
he that this one last desperate relative of mine
crazy enough to go through the agony of
couple of hundred head of cattle because
es this take care of any responsibility
a parent for teaching about you know
gives us another important economic
for continuing to own horses. ◆◆

n
that
what
justifi
year, a
for the
aptly p
As an
for ac

life v
it's t
begin
abo
obs
ha

*(Someone ripped out most of Chapters 15 & 16.
Sorry for the inconvenience.)*

87

# 17

## History Of The West (And Where Can We Find Good Politicians These Days?

As great movements go, the great westward movement in America would have to rank right up their with Beethoven's 9th and "Mississippi Squirrel Revival" by Ray Stevens. What many people forget is that in large part it, was made possible by policies of our federal government. At key times, our elected officials passed legislation which helped private citizens be rich. One example of this help is when at a critical time the federal government gave large incentives to businessmen who built a railroad all the way across the continent.

Imagine yourself, if you can, struggling along in an ox-drawn covered wagon for seven months, exposed to the wind, the rain, mosquitoes, and to other pioneers who, when nature called, had nowhere else to go than to crouch behind a 10-inch cactus. Imagine having to eat salt pork, corn-dodger, and freeze-dried camp rations day in and day out when all you had to wash them down with was rancid, cholera-infested water or warm cream soda. Imagine, due to these harsh conditions and exposure, becoming completely hardened in your response to death to the point that you could sit through a "Terminator" movie from start to finish and hang on to your cookies.

Now compare all of that to riding all of the way from St. Louis to Portland in a casino car being waited on hand and foot by courteous stewardesses who looked like Victoria Principal in her prime. It likely wouldn't even bother you to know that these luxurious accommodations were subsidized by our federal government. You can see why radical consumer groups and the wagon train industry lobbied so hard to pass legislation hostile to the Railroads. But our legislators wouldn't be swayed.

That's why it's so baffling to me that the government now days is getting so much stingier on us. Evidence of this stinginess epidemic is the wrangling about who will pay for our health care which continues unabated (meaning "without being bated" or "bateless" and not to be confused with being a reprobate, which is different). We can only hope that before someone has some kind of serious medical problem, the government will get this thing worked out.

True statesmen, the kind that I could admit that I voted for, just don't seem to be around any more. If you go back a century or so, hey now, those were politicians; real characters. In fact, at times, if you knew the right things about the right politicians, you could get the government to pay for darned near anything.

Did you know that in the late 1860s, Railroad magnates talked the government into giving them 50 million acres of prime land! What's really amazing is that unlike the money which they can just print more of, Uncle Sam didn't even really own the land when he gave it away. The weren't even finished taking it from the Indians. Today we call this creative finance.

So in order to make good on their railroad land deal, the government was forced to make squirrely deals with the uncooperative Indians, who, at the time had the clearest title by virtue of having lived there since they had driven the previous group of rival Indians off and killed them. Those cagey Indians, sensing the desperate position of the government, conned them into taking over their useless forest, beach and farm land, which then freed them up to travel on foot during cold weather to desert resort enclaves where gambling was legal and where they could finally make some really big bucks.

After it was too late, the railroads began to look around and realize how bad they had been snookered. All there was out West where they got their lands were trees which still had to be harvested, precious ores which weren't even mined yet, and lots of wide open spaces sprinkled with a few very lonely cattle ranchers.

If you were the railroads, where would you go if you wanted to find good friendly settler-type people to come from far away and live in an undeveloped wilderness with no water and no way to survive? Since Haiti didn't exist, and their was no one in Alaska at the time, they went mostly to Scandinavia and Russia where they published advertisements in all of the newspapers. In spite of the fact that the Russians couldn't read English, the pictures of the juice of plump, ripe mangos and pineapple running down the chins of bikini-clad Puget Sound area pioneer women brought settlers to the Pacific Northwest by the thousands.

Before you could say "Find somewhere else for those Red Skins", the place was crawling with settlers. Never mind that there was no water. The advertising campaign had provided thousands of great friends for all of the lonely cattle people in the area. Now they had someone to talk to besides just the cows and sheep. And this influx of new settlers didn't come a moment too soon because with all of these new farmers fencing up these places and busting up the sod, pretty soon there was no room for the horses, cows and sheep anyway, so the poor cattlemen wouldn't even have had their animals to talk to.

This statesmanship and cooperation between the federal government and big business turned out to be a great deal for everyone involved. The Congressmen all got re-elected. The railroads sold their millions of acres of ground and got rich. The cattlemen got new friends, jobs, and lives. The Indians got the desert resort properties. And the immigrants got farms...at least for a few weeks until they had to move to California where it was possible to make a living.

Now you see how much a true statesmen of the kind we had in the 1850s and 60s working with big business can accomplish. And just where do we find statesmen willing to cooperate like this who I can vote for and who will pay my health care expenses next election? ◆◆

(Emergency Square)

(Emergency Square)

(Emergency Square)

(Emergency Square)

(Emergency Square)

(Emergency Square)

Extra Page

Extra Page

Extra Page

Extra Page

Extra Page

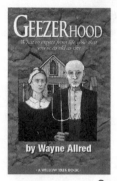
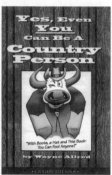